Timber Resource Statistics for Forest Land in Eastern Washington, January 2002

Andrew N. Gray, Jeremy S. Fried, Glenn Christensen, and Larry Potts

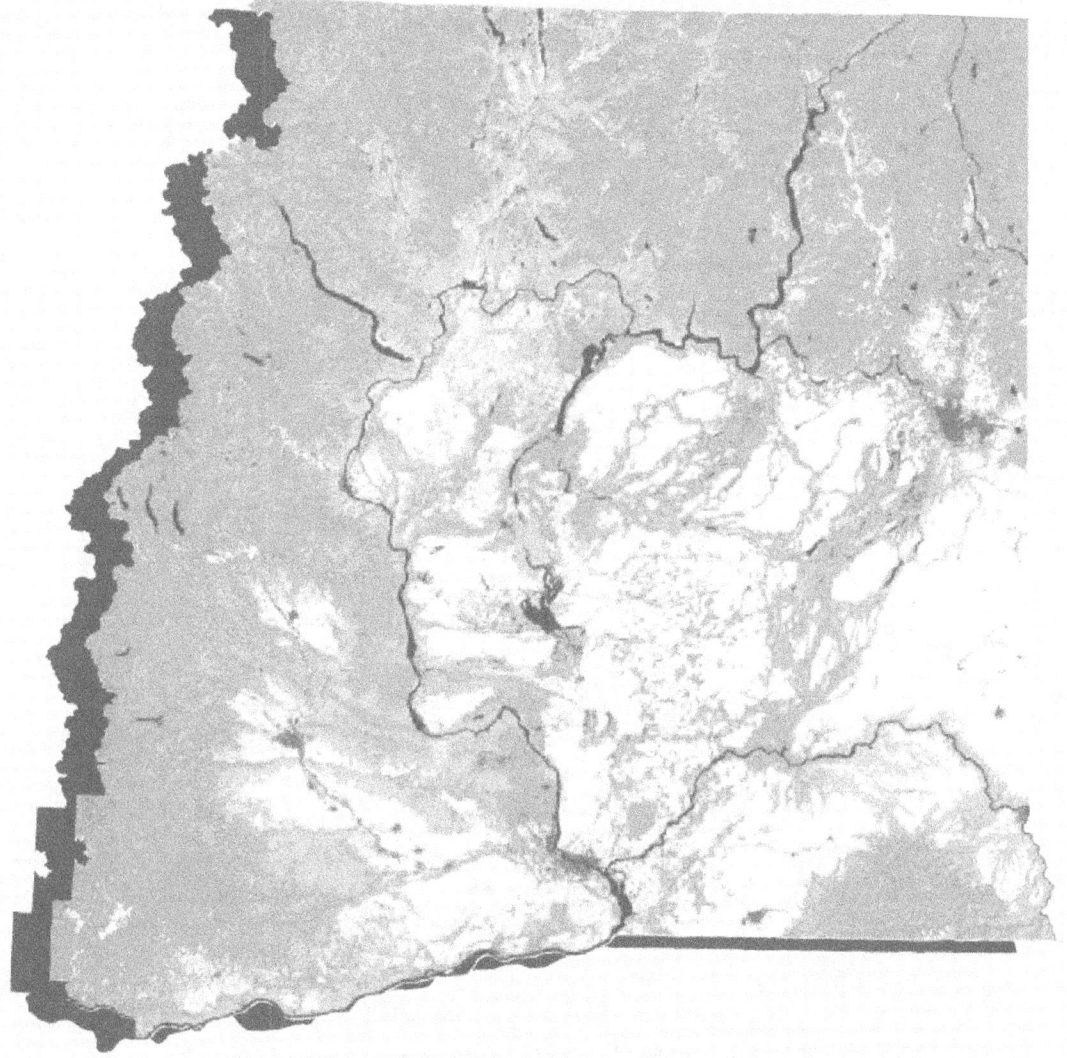

Resource Bulletin
PNW-RB-251
December 2006

 United States
Department of
Agriculture

 Forest
Service

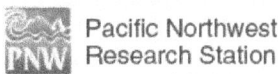 Pacific Northwest
Research Station

Authors

Andrew N. Gray is an ecologist, **Jeremy S. Fried** is a research forester, **Glenn Christensen** is a forester, and **Larry Potts** is a computer specialist, Forestry Sciences Laboratory, P.O. Box 3890, Portland, OR 97208-3890.

Cover

The image on the cover is a classified satellite image of eastern Washington from 1992 produced by the U.S. Geological Survey Multi-Resolution Land Characterization Consortium. In this representation, forest is shown in dark green, shrub-dominated areas in brown, herb-dominated areas in light green, urban areas in dark gray, agricultural areas in yellow, perennial ice and snow in white, bare ground in light gray, and water in blue.

Abstract

Gray, Andrew N.; Fried, Jeremy S.; Christensen, Glenn; Potts, Larry. 2006.
Timber resource statistics for forest land in eastern Washington, January 2002. Resour. Bull. PNW-RB-251. Portland, OR: U.S. Department of Agriculture, Forest Service, Pacific Northwest Research Station. 46 p.

This report summarizes timber resource statistics for the 20 counties in eastern Washington. The inventory sampled all private and public lands except those administered by the National Forest System in 2001, and those that were reserved from management for wood products. Area information for parks and other reserves was obtained directly from the organizations managing these areas. Statistical tables provide estimates of land area, timber volume, growth, mortality, and harvest for eastern Washington as a whole. Estimated area of forest on non-national-forest land was 4.9 million acres, and net volume of growing stock on timberland was 8.7 billion cubic feet. Estimated annual growth on non-national-forest timberland from 1990 to 2001 was 203 million cubic feet; average annual mortality was 84 million cubic feet; average annual harvest was 288 million cubic feet.

Keywords: Forest inventory, statistics (forest), land area, land use change, timber volume, eastern Washington.

Preface

Forest Inventory and Analysis (FIA) is a nationwide program of the USDA Forest Service authorized by the Forest and Rangeland Renewable Resources Research Act of 1978. Work units at Forest Service research and experiment stations conduct forest resource inventories throughout the 50 states. The FIA Program of the Pacific Northwest Research Station in Portland, Oregon, is responsible for forest inventories in Alaska, California, Hawaii, Oregon, and Washington.

Summary

The 20 counties in eastern Washington had an estimated 21.5 million acres of land in 2001 that was not administered by the U.S. Department of Agriculture, Forest Service, National Forest System (NFS). This land is collectively referred to in the text of this report as "non-NFS." Forest land represented about 23 percent (4.9 million acres) of the non-NFS land area in eastern Washington. Timberland (forest land capable of producing industrial wood products and not reserved from management for wood products) represented 18 percent (3.9 million acres) of the non-NFS land area in eastern Washington. Forest industry owned about 21 percent of the non-NFS timberland (0.8 million acres), and the proportions for other private and other public were 61 and 18 percent (2.4 and 0.7 million acres), respectively. Net volume of growing stock was estimated as 8.7 billion cubic feet, with 97 percent in conifer species. The three species with the greatest volume were Douglas-fir (40 percent), ponderosa pine (28 percent), and grand fir (9 percent). About 28 percent of the volume was on land owned by other public owners, 14 percent by forest industry, and 58 percent by other private owners. Estimated annual growth of growing stock for non-NFS lands was 203 million cubic feet, the average annual mortality was 84 million cubic feet, and the average annual harvest was 288 million cubic feet. About 0.6 percent of the non-NFS timberland present in 1991 was converted to nonforest land uses, and 0.4 percent was newly designated as reserved.

Contents

List of Tables

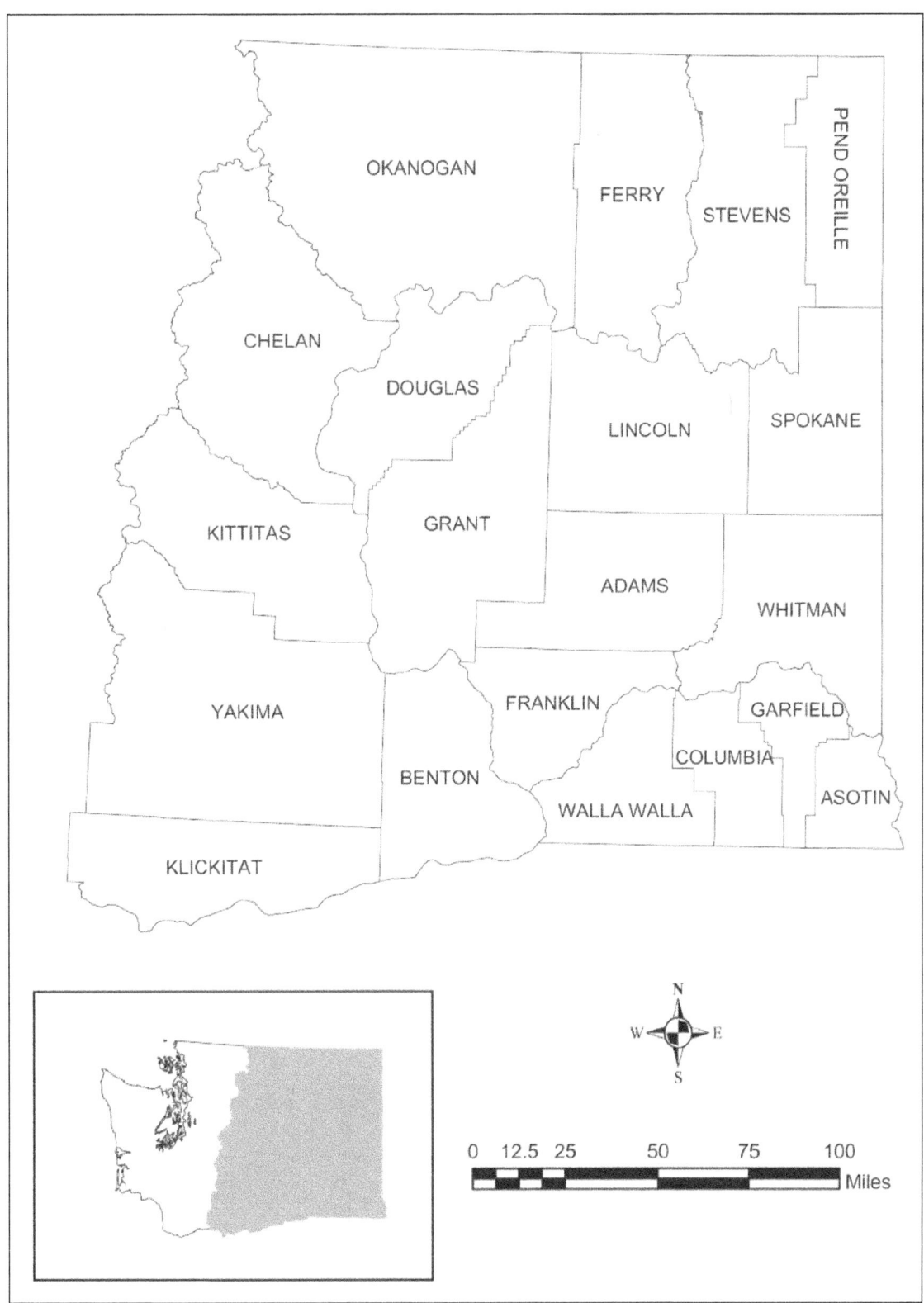

Eastern Washington Counties

Introduction

The Forest Inventory and Analysis unit of the USDA Forest Service, Pacific Northwest Research Station (PNW-FIA) conducted a multiresource inventory in the forests of eastern Washington in 2001. The inventory included all lands except those administered by the USDA Forest Service National Forest System (NFS). This report summarizes the timber resource statistics for the non-NFS forests of eastern Washington. Data collected by PNW-FIA on all forest lands beginning in 2002 will be included in a forthcoming statistical report for the entire state. Other resources sampled as part of the 2001 inventory but not included in this report are understory vegetation, insect and disease damage, and snags. These data will be incorporated in future analyses of the status of eastern Washington's forests.

Eastern Washington was first inventoried in 1935 (Cowlin and others 1942), 1953-61 (various Forest Survey reports by county), 1967-68 (Arbogast 1974, Howard 1975), 1980 (Bassett and Oswald 1983), and 1990 (McKay and others 1995). The 2001 inventory relied on a spatially-systematic sample of plot locations originally established in the early 1960s; earlier inventories were based on forest type maps.

In the late 1990s, the national FIA Program implemented several changes to the base plot grid, the timing of sampling, and the field plot design to improve national standardization and comparability across states and ownerships (Gillespie 1999). If the new annualized design had been implemented in Washington starting in 2000, there would have been a 19-year lag between completion of the last inventory in 1990 and completion of field sampling for all 10 annual panels in 2009. It was decided instead to "close out" the existing field sample design with a rapid periodic remeasurement in 2001 to provide a current estimate of forest conditions and trends. This remeasurement inventory collected less field data than the most recent inventory in 1990. The new annualized inventory design was started in Washington in 2002.

This report contains statistical tables that provide current estimates of forest land area, change estimates, number of trees, timber volume, growth, mortality, and harvest for non-Forest Service lands.

Highlights

Forest land constituted about 23 percent of the 21.5 million acres of non-NFS land in 2001 (table 1). About 80 percent of the non-NFS forest land, or 3.9 million acres, qualified as available timberland: forest land capable of producing industrial wood products and not reserved from management for wood products (see the "Terminology" section for definitions of all terms in this report). The area of timberland declined by about 1.0 percent (38,000 acres) between 1990 and 2001 (after accounting for the effect of changes in the definition of reserved lands), with 0.6 percent (22,000 acres) being converted to nonforest uses and 0.4 percent (16,000 acres) being converted to reserved categories (table 25). This rate of land conversion was a decline from the 1980-90 period, when the rate of timberland conversion was about 3.8 percent (McKay and others 1995). Some sizeable land exchanges between private and other public owners and the National Forest System in the late 1990s resulted in a net transfer of approximately 51,000 acres of land in eastern Washington to the National Forest System, primarily in Kittitas and Chelan Counties.

The harvest of timber as recorded from mill surveys for all lands in eastern Washington (including national forests) declined between the 1980s and 1990s, and shifted from public lands to privately owned lands (table 28). In the 1980s, production averaged 356, 94, and 671 million board feet per year from national forest, other public, and private lands, respectively (McKay and others 1995). In the 1990s, production averaged 150, 82, and 790 million board feet per year, respectively, for a total decline of 9 percent. For non-NFS lands, however, production in the 1990s was 14 percent greater than during the 1980s.

Reflecting the increased harvest, standing volume on non-NFS timberlands in eastern Washington declined from 9.3 to 8.7 billion cubic feet based on plots measured during the 1990 and 2001 inventories, after accounting for the effect of changes in reserve definition (table 26). Most of the decline is attributed to growth being 14 percent lower than the sum of removals and mortality. Growth was greater than the sum of mortality and removals on other public lands, but not on private lands.

The distribution of stand size classes for non-NFS timberland in eastern Washington tended to be skewed toward the small size classes. About 3 percent of the non-NFS lands had stands with a quadratic mean diameter (QMD) of 21 inches or greater ("large sawtimber"), and 35 percent had a QMD less than 9 inches ("seedling-sapling" and "poletimber") (table 7). Public lands, such as those managed by state, county, and federal agencies other than the Forest Service, had about 7 percent of the timberland area in stands with a QMD of 21 inches or greater. Forest industry and nonindustrial private owners had about 1 and 2 percent of their land in these larger diameter classes, respectively. Sixty percent of all non-NFS lands had QMDs between 9 and 21 inches.

Inventory Procedures

Eastern Washington was inventoried by using a scheme with double sampling for stratification (Cochran 1977). The sampling was implemented on a permanent systematic grid and produced an even geographic distribution of both secondary (field) and primary (photo) plots across the state. Photo plots were randomly placed within each square of the grid. However, a large area in eastern Washington was treated as a "nonforest zone," which was not sampled with primary or secondary plots.

The primary sample for the non-NFS lands of eastern Washington consisted of a grid of about 20,000 points established in 1980 and assessed by using aerial photographs taken in the late 1980s. Data collected on each point included owner group, land class, forest type, density, and stand size class. For lands that had changed to or from National Forest or reserve categories, new assessments of owner group and land class were made by using a classification of 1992 satellite imagery (USDI Geological Survey 1999) and recent digital maps of public land administrative and reserve area boundaries from the respective agencies. An entirely new primary sample was not conducted for this close-out periodic inventory for several reasons: (1) to reduce costs, (2) changes in forest cover are slower in eastern Washington than in other parts of the region, and (3) errors in classification of the predominantly multistructured forests in eastern Washington tend to reduce the contribution of the primary sample to inventory accuracy compared to other parts of the region (MacLean 1972).

The secondary sample consisted of 742 forest and nonforest field locations established in previous inventories and remeasured or reclassified in 2001. To collect the necessary data for this rapid periodic closeout inventory, the secondary sample consisted of three plots systematically selected out of every five of the base inventory grid sampled in 1990. Examination of inventory results indicated that the systematic selection resulted in a slightly different ratio of timberland plots to total plots in 2001 than in 1990, but no adjustment after the fact was made (see appendix for more information). This sample represents about a 1-in-27 subsample of the primary sample.

In 1990, a cluster of five subplots was measured at grid locations that met the definition of forest land not reserved from timber harvest. At that time, the subplots sampled a single homogeneous condition (i.e., land use class or stand type) by moving subplots from the standard configuration if necessary. Variable-radius sampling was used to select trees 5 inches diameter at breast height (d.b.h.) and greater, and a smaller fixed-radius plot was used to sample trees less than 5 inches d.b.h.

In 2000, four of the five previously measured subplots on accessible forest-land plots that remained in the same condition as the grid point (the center of subplot 1) and which met the criteria for accessible forest land not reserved from timber management were fully remeasured, including trees that grew into the fixed and variable-radius plots. Access was denied to 13 of the forest-land plots; careful examination of recent (i.e., 1- to 2-year-old) aerial photography indicated no harvest or other major disturbance had occurred on these plots, so tree growth and mortality were projected from the previously collected data by using previously measured growth rates and mortality rates derived from inventory plots that were visited. Ownership at the time of the previous inventory was updated on three plots based on new information obtained during remeasurement.

Inventory data are summarized by using various land, owner, and forest type criteria in the following tables. Definitions for some of the owner categories used by PNW-FIA differ from those used in national FIA summary publications. For example, in national publications "forest industry" only includes owners that operate wood-processing plants; in PNW-FIA reports it also includes other private owners that grow timber for industrial use. See the "Terminology" section for definitions of terms.

Land and Water Area Updated

The U.S. Department of Commerce, Bureau of the Census compiles and publishes the acreage of land and water in the United States every 10 years (U.S. Department of Commerce 2000). These area figures, available by state and county, are used as the basis for the gross number of acres to be inventoried in each county. The 1990 inventory was based on 1980 census data, and the 2001 inventory used 2000 census figures. Raster-scanned topographic maps from the USDI Geological Survey and a geographic information system were used for the newer assessment by the Bureau of the Census to identify water bodies and landforms and to determine the size of areas much smaller than was previously possible. As a result, the definition of inland water was changed to reflect the finer resolution. Streams with a minimum width of 200 feet are now recognized, compared to 660 feet in 1980; small water bodies are now at least 4.5 acres, compared to a minimum size of 40 acres before. In addition, areas covered intermittently with water were reclassified as "land." The difference in census land area by county between the 1980 and 2000 census ranged from 170 to 13,478 acres. Apparently because of the addition of acres with intermittent water, most of the changes were increases in land area in the "nonforest zone" and did not affect forest-land estimates appreciably. Estimates of non-national-forest land area were calculated by subtracting the area of national-forest-administered lands by county, as reported for 2001 (USDA Forest Service 2001).

Change in Reserved Land Definitions

The standard national definition for reserved lands used by FIA has been changed to: "Reserved land is withdrawn by law(s) prohibiting the management of land for the production of wood products (not merely controlling or prohibiting wood harvesting methods)... The prohibition against management for wood products cannot be changed through decision of the land manager (management agency) or through a change in land management personnel, but rather is permanent in nature" (USDA Forest Service 2000). In the 1990 inventory, reserved lands were lands that prohibited timber utilization (as opposed to **management** for timber production) and included lands that were administratively withdrawn at the discretion of the landowner.

For non-NFS lands, the change in definition means that lands managed by conservation groups or any other private entity (including Native American tribes) are no longer considered reserved, and public conservation lands that may occasionally harvest timber but do not include timber production in their mandate (e.g., National Wildlife Refuges) are now considered reserved. The change in definition meant, for eastern Washington, that approximately 129,000 acres of Native American lands previously considered reserved are now considered available, and 50,000 acres of National Wildlife Refuge land previously considered available are now considered reserved.

Analysis of Change Between Inventories for Non-National-Forest Lands

To analyze change in forest statistics, the 1990 data for remeasured plots were recompiled to account for technical changes in the 2000 inventory and corrections in ownership for 1990. The summaries presented in tables 25 through 27 have been developed from remeasured plots outside of national forests and include recompiled data from the 1990 inventory. Caution should be used in comparing present statistics and those published by McKay and others (1995) because of procedural changes, stratification differences, and plot changes. Comparing estimates from previous to current ones is comparing independent estimates of the resource at different points in time; although both are valid estimates, the differences between them will not be the same as the figures derived from the analyses of change on the same plots by using the same compilation procedures.

Reliability of Inventory Data

Inventories conducted by FIA are designed to provide sampling errors consistent with national standards set by the Forest Service. The target error for area of timberland is ≤3 percent per million acres and ≤10 percent per billion cubic feet of growing-stock volume.

Estimates for inventory categories that occupy large areas are more precise than estimates for small areas. Estimates for the entire inventory area are more reliable than estimates for individual counties. As estimates are made for smaller portions of the sample population, the confidence intervals increase in relation to the size of the estimate. Confidence intervals are quantitative expressions of the variability inherent in the estimation procedures for area and volume (i.e., the error in the estimate). The tabulation below indicates, for instance, a 68-percent (one standard error) chance that the true timberland area for other private owners in eastern Washington is within the range of 2,294,000 to 2,482,000 acres.

Estimates and standard errors for non-NFS timberland area, net volume, and net annual growth by owner class are:

Owner	Timberland area	Net volume	Net annual growth
	Thousand acres	*Million cubic feet*	
Other public	714 ± 62	2,464 ± 300	40 ± 6
Forest industry	830 ± 74	1,203 ± 177	44 ± 7
Other private	2,388 ± 94	5,067 ± 337	120 ± 8
All owners	3,931 ± 100	8,735 ± 464	203 ± 12

The width of confidence intervals vary with the magnitude of the estimate and the variance associated with the estimate. The tables report the sampling error for the row and column totals as percentages, calculated by dividing the standard error by the estimated value. The following is a table of approximate standard errors and sampling errors calculated by applying a regression analysis between actual standard error and the estimate involved. These regressions have r-square values greater than 0.92, indicating that 92 percent of the variance in the relation can be accounted for by the equation. The actual error estimates for the cells in each table can be obtained from the Portland FIA unit upon request, either in writing or from their Web site (http://www.fs.fed.us/pnw/fia/).

Timberland area			Growing-stock volume		
Estimate	**Interval**	**Percent**	**Estimate**	**Interval**	**Percent**
Thousand acres			*Million cubic feet*		
3,000	±101	3	6,000	±351	6
2,000	±94	5	4,000	±308	8
1,500	±89	6	2,000	±242	12
1,000	±82	8	1,000	±184	18
800	±79	10	800	±167	21
600	±74	12	600	±146	24
400	±67	17	400	±119	30
200	±55	28	200	±79	40
100	±43	43	100	±47	47
50	±32	64	50	±23	46
25	±20	80	25	±12	48

Terminology

Available other forest land—

Forest land incapable of growing 20 cubic feet per acre per year (mean annual increment at culmination in fully stocked, natural stands) of industrial wood because of adverse conditions such as sterile soils, dry climate, poor drainage, subalpine sites, steepness, or rockiness, and not in a reserved status through withdrawal of the area by laws prohibiting the management of land for the production of wood products.

Class of timber—

A classification of trees as growing stock, cull, and salvable dead. Growing-stock trees are divided into poletimber and sawtimber trees.

Condition class—

A mapped area on a plot with a distinct land class (for example, timberland, oak woodland, nonforest) or a distinct vegetative condition (for example, forest type, stand size). The first condition identified at plot center is the only condition that is remeasured and used for the analysis of periodic change.

County and municipal lands—

Lands owned by county and other local public agencies.

Cull trees—

Live trees of noncommercial species and live trees of commercial species that are more than 75-percent defective. Noncommercial species are apple, black locust, holly, junipers, Pacific yew, Pacific dogwood, white alder, and willow. Cull trees are not growing-stock trees.

Cull trees, rotten—
Cull trees with defect caused primarily by rot.

Cull trees, sound—
Trees of noncommercial species or cull trees of commercial species with defect caused primarily by poor form and roughness.

Diameter class—
A classification of trees based on diameter outside the bark measured at breast height, 4½ feet above the ground. The common abbreviation for diameter at breast height is d.b.h. Trees are grouped into 2-inch classes up to 21 inches d.b.h., after which the class intervals become broader.

Even-aged stands—
Stands where 70 percent or more of the tree stocking falls within three adjacent 10-year age classes.

Forest industry lands—
Lands owned by companies that grow timber for industrial use. Includes companies both with and without wood processing plants.

Forest land—
Land at least 10 percent stocked with live trees, or land that had this minimum tree stocking in the past and is not currently developed for nonforest use. The minimum area recognized is 1 acre; it must be 115 feet wide.

Forest types—
Stands are assigned a pure softwood, pure hardwood, or softwood-hardwood forest type. Stands with 70 percent or more of the stocking in live softwood trees are classified as pure softwood types and are assigned the type name of the softwood species with the greatest stocking among all softwoods on the condition class plot. Stands with 70 percent or more of the stocking in live hardwood trees are classified as pure hardwood types and are assigned the type name of the hardwood species with the greatest stocking among all hardwoods on the condition class plot. Mixed species types are assigned if softwood stocking is 31 to 69 percent total stocking on the plot; stands with 50 to 69 percent of the stocking in live softwood trees are classed as softwood-hardwood types and receive a type name that includes the

softwood species with the greatest softwood stocking, followed by the hardwood species with the greatest hardwood stocking; stands with 51 to 69 percent of the stocking in live hardwood trees are classed as hardwood-softwood types and receive a type name that includes the hardwood species with the greatest hardwood stocking, followed by the softwood species with the greatest softwood stocking. For ease in reporting, only the primary forest type will be identified in the summary tables

Growing-stock trees—
All live trees growing on timberland except cull trees (see "cull trees").

Growing-stock volume—
Net volume in cubic feet of live sawtimber and pole-timber growing-stock trees from the top of a stump 12 inches tall to a minimum 4-inch top (of central stem) inside the bark. Net volume is gross volume less deductions for rot and missing bole sections.

Growth, current net annual, growing stock—
The increase in growing-stock volume on timberland during the last year of the period between the previous and current inventories. Components of current net annual growth for growing-stock volume include (a) the increment in net volume of poletimber and sawtimber growing-stock trees alive at the beginning of the year and surviving to year end; plus (b) ingrowth, the net volume of growing-stock trees reaching poletimber or sawtimber size during the year; minus (c) mortality, the net volume of poletimber and sawtimber growing-stock trees that died during the year.

Growth, current net annual, sawtimber—
The increase in sawtimber volume on timberland during the last year of the period between the previous and current inventories. Components of current net annual growth for sawtimber volume include (a) the increment in net volume of sawtimber trees alive at the beginning of the year and surviving to year end; plus (b) ingrowth, the net volume of trees reaching sawtimber size during the year; minus (c) mortality, the net volume of sawtimber trees that died during the year.

Growth, periodic gross, growing stock—
The increase in growing-stock volume between the previous and current inventories that is attributable to increasing tree size. Periodic gross growth includes (a) the increment in net volume of poletimber and sawtimber growing-stock trees alive at both the previous and current inventories; (b) the increment in net volume of

poletimber and sawtimber growing-stock trees alive at the previous inventory and harvested between inventories; and (c) ingrowth, the net volume of growing-stock trees reaching poletimber or sawtimber size between inventories.

Growth, periodic gross, sawtimber—
The increase in sawtimber volume between the previous and current inventories that is attributable to increasing tree size. Periodic gross growth includes (a) the increment in net volume of sawtimber trees alive at both the previous and current inventories; (b) the increment in net volume of sawtimber trees alive at the previous inventory and harvested between inventories; and (c) ingrowth, the net volume of trees reaching sawtimber size between inventories.

Hardwoods—
Nonconiferous trees, usually broad-leaved. See "Names of Trees" for a list of hardwood species in this report.

Industrial wood—
All commercial roundwood products except fuelwood. Roundwood includes logs or bolts that are in straight sections at least 8 feet long for hardwoods and 12 feet long for softwoods.

Land area—
Area reported as land by the Bureau of the Census (U.S. Department of Commerce 2000). Total land area includes dry land and land temporarily or partially covered by water, such as marshes, swamps, and river flood plains; streams, sloughs, and canals less than 200 feet wide; and lakes, reservoirs, and ponds less than 4.5 acres.

Land class—
A classification of land by major use. The minimum area for classification is 1 acre.

Mean annual increment (MAI) at culmination—
A measure of the productivity of forest land expressed as the average increase in cubic-foot volume per acre per year. For a given species and site index, the mean is based on the age at which the MAI culminates for fully stocked natural stands. The MAI is calculated from equations and is based on the site index of the plot.

Mortality, average annual, sawtimber—
The annual net volume of sawtimber trees that died between the previous and current inventories.

National forest lands—

Federal lands that have been designated by Executive order or statute as national forest or purchase units and other lands under the administration of the U.S. Department of Agriculture, Forest Service, including experimental areas and Bankhead-Jones Title III lands.

Native American lands—

Tribal and allotted lands held in trust by the federal government. Native American lands are grouped with farmer and miscellaneous private lands as other private lands.

Net volume—

Gross volume less deductions for sound and rotten defects. Growing-stock net volume is gross cubic-foot volume less deductions for rot and missing bole sections on poletimber and sawtimber growing-stock trees. Sawtimber net volume is gross board-foot volume less deductions for rot, sweep, crook, missing bole sections, and other defects that affect the use of sawtimber trees for lumber.

Noncommercial species—

A tree species not suitable for industrial wood products: apple, black locust, holly, junipers, Pacific yew, Pacific dogwood, white alder, and willow. Noncommercial species will not be included in growing-stock volume tables; however, if one or more of these species dominate on a plot, the forest type might be classified as a noncommercial species.

Nonforest land—

Land that has never supported forests or formerly was forested and currently is developed for nonforest uses. Included are lands used for agricultural crops, Christmas tree farms, cottonwood plantations, improved pasture, residential areas, city parks, constructed roads, operating railroads and their right-of-way clearings, powerline and pipeline clearings, streams more than 30 feet wide, and 1- to 40-acre areas of water classified by the U.S. Department of Commerce, Bureau of the Census, as land. If intermingled in forest areas, unimproved roads and other non-forest strips must be more than 120 feet wide, and clearings or other areas must be 1 acre or larger to qualify as nonforest land.

Nonstocked areas—

Timberland less than 10 percent stocked with live trees. Recent clearcuts scheduled for planting are classified as nonstocked area.

Other private lands—

Private lands not owned by forest industry. Native American lands, farmer-owned lands, and miscellaneous private lands are included.

Other public lands—

Lands administered by public agencies other than the U.S. Department of Agriculture, Forest Service. Other public lands do not include Native American lands, which are included with other private lands.

Poletimber stands—

Stands with a quadratic mean diameter (mean diameter weighted by basal area) from 5.0 to 9.0 inches d.b.h. in a softwood stand and from 5.0 to 11.0 inches d.b.h. in a hardwood stand.

Poletimber trees—

Live growing-stock trees of commercial species that are 5.0 inches d.b.h. or larger but smaller than sawtimber trees.

Reserved other forest—

Forest land incapable of growing 20 cubic feet per acre per year (mean annual increment at culmination in fully stocked, natural stands) of industrial wood that is withdrawn by laws prohibiting the management of land for the production of wood products.

Reserved timberland—

Forest land capable of growing 20 cubic feet or more per acre per year (mean annual increment at culmination in fully stocked, natural stands) of industrial wood that is withdrawn by laws prohibiting the management of land for the production of wood products.

Roundwood—

Logs, bolts, or other round sections cut from trees.

Sapling and seedling stands—

Stands with a quadratic mean diameter (mean diameter weighted by basal area) less than 5.0 inches d.b.h.

Sapling and seedling trees—

Live trees of commercial species that are less than 5.0 inches d.b.h. and have no diseases, defects, or deformities likely to prevent their becoming poletimber trees.

Saw-log portion—

The bole of sawtimber trees between the stump and the saw-log top. Saw-log top is 7.0 inches in diameter outside bark on softwoods and 9.0 inches in diameter outside bark on hardwoods.

Sawtimber stands—

Stands with a quadratic mean diameter (mean diameter weighted by basal area) larger than 9.0 inches d.b.h. in a softwood stand and larger than 11.0 inches d.b.h. in a hardwood stand. Small sawtimber stands are sawtimber stands with a mean diameter (weighted by basal area) less than 21.0 inches d.b.h. Large sawtimber stands are sawtimber stands that have a mean diameter 21.0 inches or larger d.b.h.

Sawtimber trees—

Live softwood trees of commercial species at least 9.0 inches d.b.h. and live hardwood trees of commercial species at least 11.0 inches d.b.h. At least 25 percent of the board-foot volume in a sawtimber tree must be free from defect. Softwood trees must contain at least one 12-foot saw log with a top diameter of not less than 7 inches outside bark; hardwood trees must contain at least one 8-foot saw log with a top diameter of not less than 9 inches outside bark.

Sawtimber volume—

Net volume of sawtimber trees measured in board feet. Softwood volume is estimated from the top of a stump 12 inches tall up to a minimum 6-inch top diameter, inside bark, and hardwood volume is estimated from the top of a stump 12 inches tall up to a minimum 8-inch top diameter, inside bark. Net sawtimber volume equals gross volume less deduction for rot, sweep, crook, and other defects that affect use for lumber.

Scribner rule—

The common board-foot log rule used locally in eastern Washington to determine sawtimber volume. Scribner volume is estimated in terms of 16-foot logs for softwoods and hardwoods. See "sawtimber volume" for utilization limits.

Site class—

A classification of the potential productivity of forest land expressed as mean annual increment (MAI) at culmination in fully stocked natural stands, determined from site index. Six classes in this report are based on a range of MAI values that were calculated on every plot.

Site index—

A measure of the productivity of forest land expressed as the average height of dominant and codominant trees at a specified age.

Softwoods—

Coniferous trees, usually evergreen, with needles or scalelike leaves. See "Names of Trees" for a list of softwood species in this report.

Stand age—

The 10-year age class that best characterizes the stand. See "even-aged stand" and "uneven-aged stand" for more details.

Stand-size class—

A classification of stands based on tree size. Stand-size classes are sawtimber, poletimber, and sapling-seedling stands.

State lands—

Lands owned by states or administered by state agencies.

Timber harvest—

Volume of roundwood removed from forest land for products. Timber harvest statistics reported in table 28 were collected by the Washington Department of Natural Resources.

Timber volume—

Includes the net volume in cubic feet of poletimber and sawtimber trees and salvable dead sawtimber trees, and the net volume in cubic feet of cull trees of commercial species. In table 17, the volume of cull trees includes the gross volume of noncommercial species. Volume is measured from the top of a stump 12 inches tall to a minimum 4-inch top diameter, inside bark.

Timberland—

Forest land capable of growing 20 cubic feet or more per acre per year (mean annual increment at culmination in fully stocked, natural stands) of industrial wood and not in a reserved status through withdrawal of the area by laws prohibiting the management of land for the production of wood products.

Uneven-aged stands—

Stands where less than 70 percent of the tree stocking falls in three adjacent 10-year age classes.

Upper stem portion—

The bole of sawtimber trees above the saw-log top—7.0 inches diameter outside bark for softwoods and 9.0 inches diameter outside bark for hardwoods—to a minimum top diameter of 4.0 inches inside bark, or to the point where the central stem divides into limbs.

Names of Trees

Common name	Scientific name[1]
Softwoods:	
Alaska-cedar	*Chamaecyparis nootkatensis* (D. Don) Spach
Douglas-fir	*Psuedotsuga menziesii* (Mirb.) Franco
Engelmann spruce	*Picea engelmannii* Parry ex Engelm.
Grand fir	*Abies grandis* (Dougl. ex D. Don) Lindl.
Juniper	*Juniperus* spp.
Lodgepole pine	*Pinus contorta* Dougl. ex Loud.
Mountain hemlock	*Tsuga mertensiana* (Bong.) Carr.
Noble fir	*Abies procera* Rehd.
Pacific silver fir	*Abies amabilis* Dougl. ex Forbes
Pacific yew	*Taxus brevifolia* Nutt.
Ponderosa pine	*Pinus ponderosa* Dougl. ex Laws.
Sitka spruce	*Picea sitchensis* (Bong.) Carr.
Subalpine fir	*Abies lasiocarpa* (Hook.) Nutt.
Western hemlock	*Tsuga heterophylla* (Raf.) Sarg.
Western larch	*Larix occidentalis* Nutt.
Western redcedar	*Thuja plicata* Donn ex D. Don
Western white pine	*Pinus monticola* Dougl. ex D. Don
Whitebark pine	*Pinus albicaulis* Engelm.
Hardwoods:	
Apple	*Malus* spp.
Bigleaf maple	*Acer macrophyllum* Pursh
Black cottonwood	*Populus trichocarpa* Torr. & Gray
Black locust	*Robinia pseudoacacia* L.
Cherry	*Prunus* spp.
Holly	*Ilex* spp.
Oregon ash	*Fraxinus latifolia* Benth.
Oregon white oak	*Quercus garryana* Dougl. ex Hook.
Pacific dogwood	*Cornus nuttallii* Audubon
Pacific madrone	*Arbutus menzeisii* Pursh
Quaking aspen	*Populus tremuloides* Michx.
Red alder	*Alnus rubra* Bong.
Western paper birch	*Betula papyrifera* Marsh var. *commutata* (Regel) Fern.
White alder	*Alnus rhombifolia* Nutt.
Willow	*Salix* spp.

[1] Nomenclature per Little (1979).

Acknowledgments

Many people were involved in the collection of data and the design of the inventory. Thanks go to the data collection staff for field work: Brad Bolton, Chuck Brushwood, Chuck Veneklase, Carl Clemons, Perry Colclasure, R. Johnson, Mike Kazio, Kirsten Meyers, R. Miller, John Mitchell, Todd Morris, Melissa Patterson, Amanda Rollwage, Samuel Solano, Glenn Starkweather, and Andrew Wood. Thanks to Bruce Lippke, George McFadden, Todd Morgan and Kevin Ceder who provided valuable reviews. A special thanks to the many landowners who allowed field crews on their lands to visit plots and measure trees.

Metric Equivalents

1 acre = 0.405 hectare

1 acre = 4046.86 square meters

1,000 acres = 404.7 hectares

1,000 cubic feet = 28.3 cubic meters

1 cubic foot per acre = 0.07 cubic meter per hectare

1 foot = 0.3048 meter

1 inch = 2.54 centimeters

1 mile = 1.609 kilometers

Literature Cited

Arbogast, H.A. 1974. The timber resources of the Inland Empire area, Washington. Resour. Bull. PNW-50. Portland, OR: U.S. Department of Agriculture, Forest Service, Pacific Northwest Forest and Range Experiment Station. 56 p.

Bassett, P.M.; Oswald, D.D. 1983. Timber resource statistics for eastern Washington. Resour. Bull. PNW-104. Portland, OR: U.S. Department of Agriculture, Forest Service Pacific Northwest Forest and Range Experiment Station. 32 p.

Cochran, W.G. 1977. Sampling techniques. 3^d ed. New York: John Wiley & Sons. 413 p.

Cowlin, R.W.; Briegleb, P.A.; Moravets, F.L. 1942. Forest resources of the ponderosa pine region of Washington and Oregon. Misc. Publ. 490. Portland, OR: U.S. Department of Agriculture, Forest Service, Pacific Northwest Forest and Range Experiment Station. 99 p.

Gillespie, A.J.R. 1999. Rationale for a national annual forest inventory program. Journal of Forestry. 97: 16-20.

Howard, J.O. 1975. The timber resources of central Washington. Resour. Bull. PNW-45. Portland, OR: U.S. Department of Agriculture, Forest Service, Pacific Northwest Forest and Range Experiment Station. 68 p.

Little, E.L., Jr. 1979. Checklist of United States trees (native and naturalized). Agric. Handb. 541. Washington DC: United States Department of Agriculture, Forest Service. 375 p.

MacLean, C.D. 1972. Photo stratification improves Northwest timber volume estimates. Res. Note PNW-150. Portland, OR: U.S. Department of Agriculture, Forest Service, Pacific Northwest Forest and Range Experiment Station. 10 p.

McKay, N.; Bassett, P.M.; MacLean, C.D. 1995. Timber resource statistics for eastern Washington. Resour. Bull. PNW-RB-201. Portland, OR: U.S. Department of Agriculture, Forest Service, Pacific Northwest Research Station. 47 p.

U.S. Department of Commerce, Bureau of the Census. 2000. 2000 US Gazetteer. Washington DC. http://www.census.gov/geo/www/gazetteer/places2k.html (May 20, 2004).

U.S. Department of Agriculture, Forest Service. 2000. Forest Inventory and Analysis national core field guide, volume 1: field data collection procedures for phase 2 plots, version 1.4. Internal report. 208 p. On file with: U.S. Department of Agriculture, Forest Service, Forest Inventory and Analysis, 201 14th St., Washington DC 20250.

U.S. Department of Agriculture, Forest Service. 2001. Land Areas of the National Forest System. Washington DC. http://www.fs.fed.us/land/staff/lar/LAR01/ (September 20, 2005).

U.S. Department of the Interior, Geological Survey. 1999. Washington land cover data set, edition 1. Sioux Falls, SD. http://edcwww.cr.usgs.gov/programs/lccp/nationallandcover.html (March 14, 2001).

Table 1—Estimated non-national-forest land area by county, land class, and reserve status, eastern Washington, January 1, 2002

County	Available timberland	Reserved timberland	Available other forest	Reserved other forest	Total forest	Nonforest	Non-NFS land total
			Thousand acres				
Adams	0	0	0	0	0	1,232	1,232
Asotin	23	0	0	0	23	330	353
Benton	0	0	0	0	0	1,090	1,090
Chelan	140	15	55	12	221	321	542
Columbia	21	0	7	0	29	368	397
Douglas	0	0	0	0	0	1,165	1,165
Ferry	572	6	166	0	744	190	934
Franklin	0	0	0	0	0	795	795
Garfield	0	0	0	0	0	359	359
Grant	0	0	0	0	0	1,716	1,716
Kittitas	286	0	35	0	321	702	1,023
Klickitat	330	5	140	0	476	708	1,183
Lincoln	44	4	33	0	81	1,398	1,479
Okanogan	488	9	249	17	763	1,109	1,873
Pend Oreille	243	1	12	0	255	116	371
Spokane	248	35	76	0	359	770	1,129
Stevens	897	43	37	0	978	388	1,366
Walla Walla	16	0	0	0	16	794	811
Whitman	7	0	7	0	15	1,367	1,382
Yakima	614	1	26	0	640	1,612	2,252
Total	3,931	119	843	28	4,921	16,530	21,451

Note: totals may be off because of rounding; data subject to sampling error.

0 = less than 500 acres found.

Table 2—Estimated area of non-national-forest reserved timberland and other forest land by forest type, eastern Washington, January 1, 2002

Forest type	Reserved timberland	Other forest Available	Other forest Reserved	Total
		Thousand acres		
Softwood types:				
Douglas-fir	34	192	8	234
Engelmann spruce/subalpine fir	1	11	12	23
Ponderosa pine	45	472	0	518
Western larch	19	0	0	19
Other softwood types	11	0	8	20
Total softwood types	110	675	28	814
Hardwood types:				
Aspen	0	8	0	8
Oregon white oak	1	91	0	92
Other hardwood types	8	22	0	30
Total hardwood types	8	121	0	130
Nonstocked	0	46	0	46
All types	119	843	28	990

Note: Totals may be off because of rounding; data subject to sampling error.

0 = less than 500 acres found.

Nonstocked areas were less than 10 percent stocked with live trees.

Table 3—Estimated area of non-national-forest timberland by county and owner class, eastern Washington, January 1, 2002

County	Public				Private				All owners	
	Miscellaneous federal	State	County and municipal	Total public	Forest industry	Native American	Miscellaneous private	Total private	Total	SE
					Thousand acres					*%*
Asotin	0	0	0	0	0	0	23	23	23	51
Chelan	0	21	0	21	43	0	76	119	140	22
Columbia	0	0	0	0	14	0	7	21	21	48
Ferry	0	17	0	17	41	406	107	555	572	6
Kittitas	0	105	0	105	145	0	35	181	286	8
Klickitat	0	84	13	97	162	12	60	234	330	10
Lincoln	0	0	0	0	0	0	44	44	44	41
Okanogan	0	129	0	129	18	225	116	359	488	9
Pend Oreille	0	12	0	12	106	12	111	230	243	10
Spokane	0	16	0	16	32	0	201	232	248	11
Stevens	42	174	0	215	228	83	371	682	897	5
Walla Walla	0	0	0	0	0	0	16	16	16	100
Whitman	0	0	0	0	0	0	7	7	7	100
Yakima	0	100	0	100	40	473	0	513	614	5
Total	42	659	13	714	830	1,212	1,176	3,218	3,931	3
SE for total (%)	0	10	100	13	9	4	7	7	3	

Note: totals may be off because of rounding; data subject to sampling error; SE = sampling error.
0 = less than 500 acres found.

Table 4—Estimated area of non-national-forest timberland by forest type and owner class, eastern Washington, January 1, 2002

Forest type	Other public	Forest industry	Other private	All owners Total	SE
	- - - - - - - - - *Thousand acre*				*%*
Softwood types:					
Douglas-fir	304	376	1,034	1,715	7
Engelmann spruce	49	0	0	49	58
Grand fir	40	73	168	281	23
Logepole pine	68	33	134	235	25
Pacific yew	0	11	0	11	100
Ponderosa pine	147	173	769	1,088	10
Subline fir	14	43	33	90	44
Western larch	25	0	59	84	39
Western redcedar	11	72	52	134	28
Total softwood types	657	781	2,249	3,687	
Hardwood types:					
Bigleaf maple	0	0	21	21	100
Black cottonwood	0	0	24	24	71
Cherry	11	0	13	24	71
Oregon white oak	0	0	12	12	100
Quaking aspen	0	0	12	12	100
Red alder	14	0	0	14	100
Western paper birch	9	11	28	48	52
Total hardwood types	33	11	112	156	
Nonstocked	24	37	27	88	38
All types	714	830	2,388	3,931	
SE for total (%)	9	9	4	3	

Note: totals may be off because of rounding; data subject to sampling error; SE = sampling error.

0 = less than 500 acres found.

Nonstocked areas were less than 10 percent stocked with live trees.

Table 5—Estimated area of non-national-forest timberland by stand size class and owner class, eastern Washington, January 1, 2002

Stand size class	Other public	Forest industry	Other private	All owners Total	SE
	- - - - - - - - - *Thousand acre*				%
Seeding-sapling	43	310	552	905	11
Poletimber	96	135	254	484	16
Small sawtimber	504	339	1,497	2,341	5
Large timber	47	9	58	113	34
Nonstocked	24	37	27	88	38
All classes	714	830	2,388	3,931	
SE for total (%)	9	9	4	3	

Note: totals may be off because of rounding; data subject to sampling error; SE = sampling error.

0 = less than 500 acres found.

Nonstocked areas were less than 10 percent stocked with live trees.

Table 6—Estimated area of non-national-forest timberland by site class and owner class, eastern Washington, January 1, 2002

Owner	Site class (cubic feet) >225	165-224	120-164	85-119	50-84	20-49	All classes Total	SE
	- - - - - - - - - - - - - - - - - *Thousand acres* - - - - - - - - - - - - - - - - -							%
Other public	0	12	48	109	301	243	714	9
Forest industry	0	0	49	228	287	265	830	9
Other private	12	30	230	519	967	631	2,388	4
All owners	12	42	327	856	1,555	1,139	3,931	
SE for total (%)	100	59	21	12	8	9	3	

Note: totals may be off because of rounding; data subject to sampling error; SE = sampling error.

0 = less than 500 acres found.

Site class is the mean annual cubic foot growth per acre at culmination in fully stocked natural stands.

Table 7—Estimated area of non-national-forest timberland by forest type and stand size class, eastern Washington, January 1, 2002

Forest type	Seedling-sapling	Poletimber	Small sawtimber	Large sawtimber	All classes Total	SE
	- - - - - - - - - - - - - - - - - *Thousand acres*				- - - -	%
Softwood types:						
Douglas-fir	397	149	1,126	43	1,715	7
Engelmann spruce	0	0	29	20	49	58
Grand fir	111	24	147	0	281	23
Lodgepole pine	59	70	105	0	235	25
Pacific yew	11	0	0	0	11	100
Ponderosa pine	163	126	761	39	1,088	10
Subalpine fir	43	7	39	0	90	44
Western larch	11	32	41	0	84	39
Western redcedar	24	17	81	12	134	28
Total softwood types	819	426	2,329	113	3,687	
Hardwood types:						
Bigleaf maple	21	0	0	0	21	100
Black cottonwood	0	12	12	0	24	71
Cherry	24	0	0	0	24	71
Oregon white oak	12	0	0	0	12	100
Quacking aspen	0	12	0	0	12	100
Red alder	0	14	0	0	14	100
Western paper birch	28	20	0	0	48	52
Total hardwood types	86	58	12	0	156	
Nonstocked					88	38
All types	905	484	2,341	113	3,931	
SE for total (%)	11	16	5	34	3	

Note: totals may be off because of rounding; data subject to sampling error; SE = sampling error.

0 = less than 500 acres found.

Nonstocked areas were less than 10 percent stocked with live trees.

Table 8—Estimated number of trees on non-national-forest timberland by species and diameter class, eastern Washington, January 1, 2002

Tree species	Seedling	1.0–2.9	3.0–4.9	5.0–6.9	7.0–8.9	9.0–10.9	11.0–12.9	13.0–14.9	15.0–16.9	17.0–18.9	19.0–20.9	21.0–22.9	23.0–24.9	25.0–26.9	27.0–28.9	29.0+	Total	SE (%)
									—— Thousand trees ——									
Softwoods:																		
Douglas-fir	255,494	188,763	87,005	49,017	33,100	27,167	19,029	14,971	8,600	6,624	4,087	3,182	1,765	1,108	565	1,444	701,921	8
Engelmann spruce	4,786	5,283	2,415	0	547	1,782	1,043	898	949	267	357	119	167	144	33	105	18,896	32
Grand fir	148,468	116,386	48,709	14,091	12,418	4,691	4,028	3,384	1,749	1,523	877	383	401	313	142	248	357,810	12
Lodgepole pine	29,220	53,663	22,669	12,670	9,543	9,437	4,015	2,734	733	644	101	0	0	0	0	0	145,430	23
Mountain hemlock	0	0	0	0	0	0	401	0	202	0	0	0	0	0	0	0	603	100
Pacific silver fir	585	4,010	2,005	3,874	697	0	317	0	189	0	0	0	0	0	0	0	11,677	95
Pacific yew	3,909	2,664	0	0	0	0	0	0	0	0	0	0	0	0	0	0	6,573	68
Ponderosa pine	148,055	108,221	37,511	26,211	24,480	12,666	14,562	10,872	6,877	4,883	3,778	2,419	1,323	927	584	1,304	404,672	12
Subalpine fir	35,829	31,960	8,685	4,547	3,293	1,073	1,057	333	308	0	0	59	0	0	0	0	87,143	29
Western hemlock	1,698	2,005	1,171	1,326	452	541	240	325	82	73	0	0	86	28	0	0	8,027	46
Western larch	17,230	38,051	13,070	10,105	4,624	5,333	3,114	1,708	815	606	936	160	217	83	96	98	96,245	23
Western red cedar	13,300	43,106	12,465	9,156	4,480	2,595	2,108	544	1,156	527	311	232	189	141	25	150	90,485	36
Western white pine	3,176	0	2,942	850	0	0	191	0	0	75	0	46	68	0	0	0	7,349	60
Whitebark pine	0	0	0	0	0	0	0	0	0	0	0	61	0	0	0	0	61	100
Total softwoods	661,749	594,112	238,648	131,847	93,634	65,284	50,104	35,769	21,659	15,222	10,448	6,662	4,216	2,745	1,445	3,349	1,936,893	
Hardwoods:																		
Bigleaf maple	896	3,752	0	0	0	0	190	0	0	0	0	0	0	0	0	0	4,838	77
Black cottonwood	951	0	0	509	1,102	526	412	353	0	0	59	48	103	0	29	25	4,119	56
Cherry	3,022	784	3,724	784	0	0	0	0	0	0	0	0	0	0	0	0	8,313	58
Oregon white oak	9,443	2,749	5,813	3,847	585	208	0	0	113	0	0	0	0	0	0	0	22,759	37
Pacific dogwood	0	0	1,108	1,069	0	0	0	0	0	0	0	0	0	0	0	0	2,177	100
Quaking aspen	6,541	1,078	3,342	575	941	861	1,529	136	407	0	0	0	61	0	0	0	15,471	42
Red alder	0	1,089	1,089	2,176	413	263	193	0	98	79	0	62	0	43	0	32	5,538	61
Western paper birch	10,773	755	5,897	5,309	2,229	409	148	0	0	0	51	0	0	0	0	0	25,572	39
Willow	0	5,121	5,171	955	915	315	414	0	0	0	0	0	0	0	0	0	12,891	53
Other hardwoods	0	951	2,854	2,576	0	0	0	0	0	0	0	0	0	0	0	0	6,381	72
Total hardwoods	31,627	16,280	28,998	17,800	6,186	2,582	2,886	489	618	79	110	110	164	43	29	57	108,057	
Total	693,376	610,391	267,646	149,647	99,820	67,866	52,990	36,258	22,277	15,301	10,558	6,772	4,381	2,788	1,474	3,406	2,044,950	
SE for total (%)	7	11	9	10	9	8	8	8	8	9	10	10	11	14	18	16		5

Note: totals may be off because of rounding; data subject to sampling error; SE = sampling error

0 = fewer than 500 trees found

Table 9—Estimated net volume of growing-stock trees on non-national-forest timberland by species and diameter class, eastern Washington, January 1, 2002

Tree species	Diameter class (inches at breast height)													All classes	
	5.0-6.9	7.0-8.9	9.0-10.9	11.0-12.9	13.0-14.9	15.0-16.9	17.0-18.9	19.0-20.9	21.0-22.9	23.0-24.9	25.0-26.9	27.0-28.9	29.0+	Total	SE %
	Million cubic feet														
Softwoods:															
Douglas-fir	100	200	308	356	403	335	346	285	264	181	146	88	463	3,474	10
Engelmann spruce	0	3	28	24	36	47	16	25	12	20	21	7	31	271	36
Grand fir	34	76	53	80	106	79	90	55	34	50	45	25	65	792	17
Lodgepole pine	40	75	134	92	88	32	40	7	0	0	0	0	0	507	23
Mountain hemlock	0	0	0	6	0	7	0	0	0	0	0	0	0	12	100
Pacific silver fir	3	5	0	6	0	9	0	0	0	0	0	0	0	23	100
Ponderosa pine	43	113	127	235	281	258	261	253	205	145	122	93	299	2,435	9
Subalpine fir	6	22	10	18	11	14	0	0	5	0	0	0	0	86	40
Western hemlock	2	4	5	5	13	4	6	0	0	11	4	0	0	54	47
Western larch	24	34	73	72	49	37	38	74	11	25	14	18	18	486	16
Western redcedar	24	23	29	39	14	42	27	20	19	17	15	3	42	314	26
Western white pine	2	0	0	4	0	0	5	0	5	10	0	0	0	25	51
Whitebark pine	0	0	0	0	0	0	0	0	5	0	0	0	0	5	100
Total softwoods	277	555	767	936	1,002	864	828	720	560	459	367	234	918	8,485	
Hardwoods:															
Bigleaf maple	0	0	0	3	0	0	0	0	0	0	0	0	0	3	100
Black cottonwood	1	12	9	10	11	0	0	0	4	10	0	1	3	62	59
Cherry	2	0	0	0	0	0	0	0	0	0	0	0	0	2	100
Oregon white oak	12	5	3	0	0	4	0	0	0	0	0	0	0	23	49
Quaking aspen	3	9	14	31	4	18	0	0	0	6	0	0	0	85	65
Red alder	5	2	0	3	0	4	3	3	0	0	0	0	0	20	83
Western paper birch	15	15	5	4	0	0	0	2	0	0	0	0	0	41	33
Willow	1	4	3	6	0	0	0	0	0	0	0	0	0	13	71
Total hardwoods	38	48	34	57	15	26	3	2	7	16	0	1	3	250	
All species	315	603	801	993	1,018	889	831	721	567	475	367	235	920	8,735	
SE for total (%)	10	9	9	8	8	9	10	10	11	12	14	19	23	5	

Note: totals may be off because of rounding; data subject to sampling error; SE = sampling error.

0 = less than 500,000 cubic feet found.

Includes growing-stock trees (noncull trees of commercial species) 5.0 inches in d.b.h. and larger.

Table 10—Estimated net volume of sawtimber on non-national-forest timberland by species and diameter class, eastern Washington, January 1, 2002

Tree species	Diameter class (inches at breast height)											All classes	
	9.0-10.9	11.0-12.9	13.0-14.9	15.0-16.9	17.0-18.9	19.0-20.9	21.0-22.9	23.0-24.9	25.0-26.9	27.0-28.9	29.0+	Total	SE %
	— — — — — — — — — — — — — — — Million board feet, Scribner rule — — — — — — — — — — — — — — —												
Softwoods:													
Douglas-fir	994	1,415	1,781	1,592	1,728	1,492	1,401	984	829	507	2,796	15,519	11
Engelmann spruce	97	102	178	238	81	121	65	109	119	40	178	1,327	36
Grand fir	162	326	490	393	458	287	185	279	260	140	359	3,340	19
Lodgepole pine	455	379	381	157	211	38	0	0	0	0	0	1,621	25
Mountain Hemlock	0	19	0	31	0	0	0	0	0	0	0	50	100
Pacific silver fir	0	24	0	41	0	0	0	0	0	0	0	65	100
Ponderosa pine	393	888	1,213	1,217	1,316	1,312	1,097	801	694	541	1,797	11,270	10
Subalpine fir	26	69	51	66	0	0	27	0	0	0	0	240	44
Western hemlock	16	19	64	21	34	0	0	44	22	0	0	220	49
Western larch	244	302	214	183	193	397	56	133	78	104	92	1,998	18
Western redcedar	93	152	60	197	130	98	98	83	70	15	198	1,192	30
Western white pine	0	16	0	0	24	0	26	62	0	0	0	129	56
Whitebark pine	0	0	0	0	0	0	25	0	0	0	0	25	100
Total softwoods	2,480	3,711	4,433	4,137	4,176	3,744	2,982	2,496	2,071	1,347	5,420	36,997	
Hardwoods:													
Bigleaf maple	0	12	0	0	0	0	0	0	0	0	0	12	100
Black cottonwood	0	39	48	0	0	0	20	51	0	5	12	175	54
Oregon white oak	0	0	0	9	0	0	0	0	0	0	0	9	100
Quaking aspen	0	100	20	80	0	0	0	33	0	0	0	233	55
Red alder	0	9	0	16	14	0	7	0	0	0	0	46	100
Western paper birch	0	13	0	0	0	9	0	0	0	0	0	22	72
Willow	0	17	0	0	0	0	0	0	0	0	0	17	100
Total hardwoods	0	190	68	105	14	9	28	84	0	5	12	513	
All species	2,480	3,901	4,500	4,242	4,189	3,753	3,009	2,580	2,071	1,351	5,432	37,509	6
SE for total (%)	9	8	8	9	10	11	11	12	14	19	23		

Note: totals may be off because of rounding; data subject to sampling error; SE = sampling error.

0 = less than 500,000 board feet found.

Includes softwood sawtimber trees 9.0 inches in d.b.h. and larger, and hardwood sawtimber trees 11.0 inches in d.b.h. and larger.

Table 11—Estimated net volume of growing-stock trees on non-national-forest timberland by tree species and owner class, eastern Washington, January 1, 2002

Forest type	Other public	Forest industry	Other private	All owners Total	All owners SE
	- - - - - - - - *Million cubic feet*				*%*
Softwoods:					
Douglas-fir	1,058	488	1,929	3,474	10
Engelmann spruce	167	12	92	271	36
Grand fir	244	141	407	792	17
Lodgepole pine	157	69	281	507	23
Mountain hemlock	0	0	12	12	10
Pacific silver fir	0	0	23	23	100
Ponderosa pine	448	265	1,721	2,435	9
Subalpine fir	46	2	38	86	40
Western hemlock	6	17	31	54	47
Western larch	149	68	269	486	16
Western redcedar	117	96	101	314	26
Western white pine	10	9	6	25	51
Whitebark pine	5	0	0	5	100
Total softwoods	2,406	1,167	4,912	8,485	
Hardwoods:					
Bigleaf maple	3	0	0	3	100
Black cottonwood	1	4	56	62	59
Cherry	0	0	2	2	100
Oregon white oak	0	13	10	23	49
Quaking aspen	16	0	70	85	65
Red alder	20	0	0	20	83
Western paper birch	10	14	17	41	33
Willow	8	4	1	13	71
Total hardwoods	59	36	155	250	
All species	2,464	1,203	5,067	8,735	
SE for total (%)	12	15	7	5	

Note: totals may be off because of rounding; data subject to sampling error; SE = sampling error.

0 = less than 500,000 cubic feet found.

Includes growing stock trees (noncull trees of commercial species) 5.0 inches in d.b.h. and larger.

Table 12—Estimated net volume of sawtimber on non-national-forest timberland by tree species and owner class, eastern Washington, January 1, 2002

Forest type	Other public	Forest industry	Other private	All owners Total	SE
	- - - Million board feet, Scribner rule				%
Softwoods:					
Douglas-fir	5,248	1,971	8,300	15,519	11
Engelmann spruce	822	60	445	1,327	36
Grand fir	998	445	1,897	3,340	19
Lodgepole pine	443	191	987	1,621	25
Mountain hemlock	0	0	50	50	100
Pacific silver fir	0	0	65	65	100
Ponderosa pine	2,161	1,064	8,045	11,270	10
Subalpine fir	140	0	100	240	44
Western hemlock	25	48	147	220	49
Western larch	624	245	1,128	1,998	18
Western redcedar	475	378	339	1,192	30
Western white pine	59	46	24	129	56
Whitebark pine	25	0	0	25	100
Total softwoods	11,022	4,448	21,526	36,997	
Hardwoods:					
Bigleaf maple	12	0	0	12	100
Black cottonwood	0	22	153	175	54
Oregon white oak	0	9	0	9	100
Quaking aspen	64	0	169	233	55
Red alder	46	0	0	46	100
Western paper birch	9	0	13	22	72
Willow	17	0	0	17	100
Total hardwoods	147	30	335	513	
All species	11,169	4,479	21,862	37,509	
SE for total (%)	14	16	7	6	

Note: totals may be off because of rounding; data subject to sampling error; SE = sampling error.

0 = less than 500,000 board feet found.

Includes softwood sawtimber trees 9.0 inches in d.b.h. and larger, and hardwood sawtimber trees 11.0 inches in d.b.h. and larger.

Table 13—Estimated net volume of growing-stock trees on non-national-forest timberland by forest type and stand size class, eastern Washington, January 1, 2002

Forest type	Seedling-sapling	Poletimber	Small sawtimber	Large sawtimber	All classes Total	SE
	--		*Million cubic feet*			%
Softwood types:						
Douglas-fir	228	278	3,470	444	4,419	11
Engelmann spruce	0	0	147	83	230	57
Grand fir	47	39	386	0	472	37
Lodgepole pine	22	145	349	0	515	33
Ponderosa pine	65	90	1,888	87	2,130	12
Subalpine fir	10	13	153	0	176	66
Western larch	8	64	139	0	211	44
Western redcedar	6	38	242	34	321	35
Total softwood types	385	667	6,773	649	8,475	
Hardwood types:						
Bigleaf maple	19	0	0	0	19	100
Black cottonwood	0	31	45	0	76	72
Cherry	7	0	0	0	7	100
Oregon white oak	4	0	0	0	4	100
Quaking aspen	0	55	0	0	55	100
Red alder	0	21	0	0	21	100
Western paper birch	11	59	0	0	70	61
Total hardwood types	42	166	45	0	252	
Nonstocked					8	70
All types	427	833	6,818	649	8,735	
SE for total (%)	15	18	7	42	5	

Note: totals may be off because of rounding; data subject to sampling error; SE = sampling error.

0 = less than 500,000 cubic feet found.

Includes growing stock trees (noncull trees of commercial species) 5.0 inches in d.b.h. and larger.

Nonstocked areas were less than 10 percent stocked with live trees.

Table 14—Estimated net volume of sawtimber on non-national-forest timberland by forest type and stand size class, eastern Washington, January 1, 2002

Forest type	Seedling-sapling	Poletimber	Small sawtimber	Large sawtimber	All classes Total	SE
			Million board feet, Scribner rule			*%*
Softwood types:						
Douglas-fir	811	665	15,539	2,471	19,485	12
Engelmann spruce	0	0	614	428	1,042	57
Grand fir	165	139	1,825	0	2,129	40
Lodgepole pine	90	292	1,263	0	1,646	38
Ponderosa pine	234	213	8,679	472	9,598	13
Subalpine fir	32	40	662	0	735	68
Western larch	12	164	636	0	813	50
Western redcedar	7	87	1,030	180	1,304	35
Total softwood types	1,352	1,601	30,248	3,550	36,751	
Hardwood types:						
Bigleaf maple	105	0	0	0	105	100
Black cottonwood	0	40	201	0	241	85
Cherry	40	0	0	0	40	100
Oregon white oak	7	0	0	0	7	100
Quaking aspen	0	103	0	0	103	100
Red alder	0	63	0	0	63	100
Western paper birch	41	121	0	0	162	56
Total hardwood types	193	327	201	0	721	
Nonstocked					37	73
All types	1,545	1,928	30,449	3,550	37,509	
SE for total (%)	17	19	7	43	6	

Note: totals may be off because of rounding; data subject to sampling error; SE = sampling error.

0 = less than 500,000 board feet found.

Includes softwood sawtimber trees 9.0 inches in d.b.h. and larger, and hardwood sawtimber trees 11.0 inches in d.b.h. and larger.

Nonstocked areas were less than 10 percent stocked with live trees.

Table 15—Estimated net volume of growing-stock trees on non-national-forest timberland by forest type and owner class, eastern Washington, January 1, 2002

Forest type	Other public	Forest industry	Other private	All owners Total	SE
	- - - - - - - - *Million cubic feet*				*%*
Softwood types:					
Douglas-fir	1,357	673	2,389	4,419	11
Engelmann spruce	230	0	0	230	57
Grand fir	162	47	264	472	37
Lodgepole pine	177	72	266	515	33
Ponderosa pine	357	238	1,535	2,130	12
Subalpine fir	50	10	116	176	66
Western larch	32	0	179	211	44
Western redcedar	47	127	147	321	35
Total softwood types	2,413	1,167	4,895	8,475	
Hardwood types:					
Bigleaf maple	0	0	19	19	100
Black cottonwood	0	0	76	76	72
Cherry	0	0	7	7	100
Oregon white oak	0	0	4	4	100
Quaking aspen	0	0	55	55	100
Red alder	21	0	0	21	100
Western paper birch	30	28	11	70	61
Total hardwood types	52	28	172	252	
Nonstocked	0	8	0	8	70
All types	2,464	1,203	5,067	8,735	
SE for total (%)	12	15	7	5	

Note: totals may be off because of rounding; data subject to sampling error; SE = sampling error.

0 = less than 500,000 cubic feet found.

Includes growing stock trees (noncull trees of commercial species) 5.0 inches in d.b.h. and larger.

Nonstocked areas were less than 10 percent stocked with live trees.

Table 16—Estimated net volume of sawtimber on non-national-forest timberland by forest type and owner class, eastern Washington, January 1, 2002

Forest type	Other public	Forest industry	Other private	All owners Total	SE
	- - - - *Million board feet, Scribner rule*				%
Softwood types:					
Douglas-fir	6,574	2,624	10,287	19,485	12
Engelmann spruce	1,042	0	0	1,042	57
Grand fir	747	146	1,236	2,129	40
Lodgepole pine	573	116	957	1,646	38
Ponderosa pine	1,636	901	7,062	9,598	13
Subalpine fir	212	32	490	735	68
Western larch	70	0	742	813	50
Western redcedar	185	568	551	1,304	35
Total softwood types	11,039	4,387	21,324	36,751	
Hardwood types:					
Bigleaf maple	0	0	105	105	100
Black cottonwood	0	0	241	241	85
Cherry	0	0	40	40	100
Oregon white oak	0	0	7	7	100
Quaking aspen	0	0	103	103	100
Red alder	63	0	0	63	100
Western paper birch	67	54	41	162	56
Total hardwood types	129	54	537	721	
Nonstocked	0	37	0	37	73
All types	11,169	4,479	21,862	37,509	
SE for total (%)	14	16	7	6	

Note: totals may be off because of rounding; data subject to sampling error; SE = sampling error.

0 = less than 500,000 board feet found.

Includes softwood sawtimber trees 9.0 inches in d.b.h. and larger, and hardwood sawtimber trees 11.0 inches in d.b.h. and larger.

Nonstocked areas were less than 10 percent stocked with live trees.

Table 17—Estimated net volume of trees on non-national-forest timberland by class of timber and species group, eastern Washington, January 1, 2002

Class of timber	Softwood species	Hardwood species	All species	
			Total	SE
	Million cubic feet			%
Growing-stock trees:				
Sawtimber trees-				
Saw-log portion	7,392	109	7,501	6
Upper stem portion	261	20	282	6
Total, sawtimber	7,653	130	7,783	
Poletimber trees	832	120	952	9
All growing-stock trees	8,485	250	8,735	
Cull trees:				
Sound cull	13	8	21	42
Rotten cull	25	13	37	36
Total, cull trees	38	21	58	
All timber	8,523	270	8,793	
SE for total (%)	5	29	5	

Note: totals may be off because of rounding; data subject to sampling error; SE = sampling error.

0 = less than 500,000 cubic feet found.

Includes live trees 5.0 inches in d.b.h. and larger; sound cull includes trees of noncommercial species.

Table 18—Estimated current net annual volume growth of growing-stock trees on non-national-forest timberland by forest type and owner class, eastern Washington, January 1, 2002

Forest type	Other public	Forest industry	Other private	All owners Total	SE
	-------- Thousand cubic feet				%
Softwood types:					
Douglas-fir	23,041	26,218	59,507	108,767	10
Engelmann spruce	-505	0	0	-505	100
Grand fir	2,084	1,970	5,205	9,259	29
Lodgepole pine	2,320	1,083	5,869	9,271	30
Ponderosa pine	8,649	9,346	36,812	54,807	12
Subalpine fir	1,372	340	851	2,563	64
Western larch	1,357	0	6,132	7,490	46
Western redcedar	500	4,012	2,760	7,272	32
Total softwood types	38,818	42,969	117,136	198,923	
Hardwood types:					
Bigleaf maple	0	0	261	261	100
Black cottonwood	0	0	2,194	2,194	99
Cherry	0	0	181	181	100
Oregon white oak	0	0	80	80	100
Quaking aspen	0	0	-140	-140	100
Red alder	673	0	0	673	100
Western paper birch	191	475	225	891	60
Total hardwood types	864	475	2,800	4,139	
Nonstocked	0	153	0	153	112
All types	39,682	43,597	119,937	203,216	
SE for total (%)	14	16	7	6	

Note: totals may be off because of rounding; data subject to sampling error; SE = sampling error.

0 = less than 500 cubic feet found.

Includes growing stock trees (noncull trees of commercial species) 5.0 inches in d.b.h. and larger.

Nonstocked areas were less than 10 percent stocked with live trees.

Table 19—Estimated current net annual volume growth of sawtimber on non-national-forest timberland by forest type and owner class, eastern Washington, January 1, 2002

Forest type	Other public	Forest industry	Other private	All owners Total	SE
	- - - - - Thousand board feet, Scribner rule				%
Softwood types:					
Douglas-fir	153,918	131,542	343,300	628,760	11
Engelmann spruce	934	0	0	934	100
Grand fir	9,699	10,399	35,038	55,136	38
Lodgepole pine	14,046	1,161	33,960	49,167	40
Ponderosa pine	37,310	42,934	203,653	283,897	12
Subalpine fir	7,710	1,703	6,842	16,255	57
Western larch	2,126	0	23,574	25,700	54
Western redcedar	2,081	17,997	11,185	31,263	33
Total softwood types	227,824	205,736	657,552	1,091,112	
Hardwood types:					
Bigleaf maple	0	0	1,926	1,926	100
Black cottonwood	0	0	5,318	5,318	77
Cherry	0	0	1,197	1,197	100
Oregon white oak	0	0	236	236	100
Quaking aspen	0	0	847	847	100
Red alder	1,776	0	0	1,776	100
Western paper birch	1,313	1,590	1,438	4,341	53
Total hardwood types	3,089	1,590	10,962	15,641	
Nonstocked	0	929	0	929	94
All types	230,914	208,255	668,514	1,107,683	
SE for total (%)	13	18	8	6	

Note: totals may be off because of rounding; data subject to sampling error; SE = sampling error.

0 = less than 500 board feet found.

Includes softwood sawtimber trees 9.0 inches in d.b.h. and larger, and hardwood sawtimber trees 11.0 inches in d.b.h. and larger.

Nonstocked areas were less than 10 percent stocked with live trees.

Table 20—Estimated average annual mortality volume of growing-stock trees on non-national-forest timberland by forest type and owner class, eastern Washington, January 1, 2002

Forest type	Other public	Forest industry	Other private	All owners Total	SE
	- - - - - - - - Thousand cubic feet				%
Softwood types:					
Douglas-fir	13,571	7,392	20,071	41,035	12
Engelmann spruce	3,230	0	0	3,230	68
Grand fir	1,888	393	4,495	6,775	44
Lodgepole pine	2,478	1,067	3,831	7,376	35
Ponderosa pine	2,090	1,358	8,951	12,398	15
Subalpine fir	898	34	1,658	2,589	66
Western larch	552	0	2,059	2,611	43
Western redcedar	483	935	1,611	3,030	41
Total softwood types	25,191	11,178	42,675	79,044	
Hardwood types:					
Bigleaf maple	0	0	172	172	100
Black cottonwood	0	0	1,806	1,806	71
Cherry	0	0	43	43	100
Oregon white oak	0	0	111	111	100
Quaking aspen	0	0	1,531	1,531	100
Red alder	405	0	0	405	100
Western paper birch	436	482	199	1,117	60
Total hardwood types	841	482	3,863	5,185	
Nonstocked	0	141	0	141	94
All types	26,032	11,801	46,537	84,371	
SE for total (%)	14	18	9	7	

Note: totals may be off because of rounding; data subject to sampling error; SE = sampling error.

0 = less than 500 cubic feet found

Includes growing stock trees (noncull trees of commercial species) 5.0 inches in d.b.h. and larger.

Nonstocked areas were less than 10 percent stocked with live trees.

Table 21—Estimated average annual mortality volume of sawtimber on non-national-forest timberland by forest type and owner class, eastern Washington, January 1, 2002

Forest type	Other public	Forest industry	Other private	All owners Total	SE
	- - - -*Thousand board feet, Scribner rule*				*%*
Softwood types:					
Douglas-fir	61,317	27,286	78,733	167,335	13
Engelmann spruce	13,944	0	0	13,944	67
Grand fir	7,632	847	21,397	29,876	48
Lodgepole pine	7,494	1,691	13,288	22,472	41
Ponderosa pine	8,860	3,761	35,819	48,441	17
Subalpine fir	3,591	15	7,113	10,719	70
Western larch	1,102	0	8,354	9,456	51
Western redcedar	1,960	4,289	6,657	12,905	42
Total softwood types	105,900	37,888	171,360	315,149	
Hardwood types:					
Bigleaf maple	0	0	937	937	100
Black cottonwood	0	0	5,393	5,393	81
Cherry	0	0	244	244	100
Oregon white oak	0	0	160	160	100
Quaking aspen	0	0	2,900	2,900	100
Red alder	1,128	0	0	1,128	100
Western paper birch	542	701	651	1,893	55
Total hardwood types	1,670	701	10,284	12,655	
Nonstocked	0	721	0	721	96
All types	107,570	39,310	181,645	328,525	
SE for total (%)	15	21	10	8	

Note: totals may be off because of rounding; data subject to sampling error; SE = sampling error.

0 = less than 500 board feet found.

Includes softwood sawtimber trees 9.0 inches in d.b.h. and larger, and hardwood sawtimber trees 11.0 inches in d.b.h. and larger.

Nonstocked areas were less than 10 percent stocked with live trees.

Resource Bulletin PNW-RB-251

Table 22—Estimated area, net volume of growing stock, and net volume of sawtimber on non-national-forest timberland, by stand age and owner class, eastern Washington, January 1, 2002

Stand age	Other public			Forest industry			Other private			All owners		
	Area	Growing-stock volume	Saw-timber volume	Area	Growing-stock volume	Saw-timber volume	Area	Growing-stock volume	Saw-timber volume	Area	Growing-stock volume	Saw-timber volume
	Thousand acres	Million cubic feet	Million board feet	Thousand acres	Million cubic feet	Million board feet	Thousand acres	Million cubic feet	Million board feet	Thousand acres	Million cubic feet	Million board feet
0-9	11	0	0	50	26	76	111	62	265	172	89	341
10-19	0	0	0	186	64	244	191	47	172	377	110	416
20-29	23	26	115	35	2	0	207	181	620	265	208	735
30-39	36	57	172	26	13	44	84	112	450	146	182	666
40-49	34	27	66	73	123	431	103	95	291	211	245	789
50-59	30	64	290	76	157	634	236	407	1,575	342	628	2,499
60-69	82	242	1,017	76	190	652	250	659	2,527	409	1,091	4,197
70-79	63	149	596	103	256	938	341	783	3,465	507	1,189	5,000
80-89	44	315	1,506	102	140	492	294	806	3,494	440	1,261	5,492
90-99	126	441	1,782	36	62	277	247	852	3,914	410	1,355	5,974
100-109	61	221	989	52	150	578	95	290	1,290	208	660	2,857
110-119	36	159	724	0	0	0	46	169	819	82	328	1,543
120-129	34	130	546	0	0	0	48	196	936	82	326	1,482
130-139	0	0	0	0	0	0	0	0	0	0	0	0
140-149	14	103	557	0	0	0	0	0	0	14	103	557
150-159	21	67	293	0	0	0	0	0	0	21	67	293
160-169	13	75	410	0	0	0	0	0	0	13	75	410
170-179	0	0	0	0	0	0	14	32	162	14	32	162
180-189	0	0	0	0	0	0	0	0	0	0	0	0
190-199	20	83	428	0	0	0	26	109	572	46	193	1,000
200-299	41	305	1,677	2	21	112	41	101	496	83	427	2,286
300+	0	0	0	0	0	0	26	166	812	26	166	812
Nonstocked	24	0	0	13	0	0	27	0	0	64	0	0
Total, all ages	714	2,464	11,169	830	1,203	4,479	2,388	5,067	21,862	3,931	8,735	37,509
SE for total (%)	9	12	14	9	15	16	4	7	7	3	5	6

Note: totals may be off because of rounding; data subject to sampling error; SE = sampling error.
0 = less than 500 acres, 500,000 cubic feet, or 500,000 board feet found.
Growing-stock volume includes noncull trees of commercial species 5.0 inches d.b.h. and larger
Sawtimber volume is in Scribner rule and includes softwood sawtimber trees 9.0 inches in d.b.h. and larger, and hardwood sawtimber trees 11.0 inches in d.b.h. and larger.
Nonstocked areas were less than 10 percent stocked with live trees.

Table 23—Estimated gross annual growth, average annual mortality, and average annual removals of growing stock on non-national-forest timberland, by species and owner class, eastern Washington, January 1, 2002

Thousand cubic feet

Species	Other public			Forest industry			Other private			All owners		
	Current gross annual growth	Average annual mortality	Average annual removals	Current gross annual growth	Average annual mortality	Average annual removals	Current gross annual growth	Average annual mortality	Average annual removals	Current gross annual growth	Average annual mortality	Average annual removals
Softwoods:												
Douglas-fir	29,494	9,314	7,579	26,891	4,029	59,971	71,422	13,851	60,355	127,807	27,193	127,905
Engelmann spruce	1,595	1,909	0	414	6	480	1,484	696	0	3,493	2,611	480
Grand fir	9,666	4,608	1,953	6,784	2,539	14,062	16,354	8,036	36,451	32,804	15,183	52,466
Lodgepole pine	5,800	2,684	2,928	1,936	1,115	9,258	7,825	4,997	10,232	15,560	8,796	22,417
Mountain hemlock	0	0	0	0	0	0	234	6	0	234	6	0
Pacific silver fir	0	0	0	0	0	0	1,840	565	0	1,840	565	0
Ponderosa pine	8,917	2,130	2,016	9,808	1,640	14,692	44,997	9,358	45,499	63,723	13,129	62,208
Subalpine fir	2,014	695	0	116	23	753	1,255	800	0	3,385	1,518	753
Western hemlock	129	3	0	1,589	95	1,061	654	279	0	2,371	377	1,061
Western larch	3,567	2,327	1,602	3,330	1,138	8,841	10,101	3,245	6,161	16,998	6,710	16,604
Western redcedar	2,293	273	693	3,324	133	1,257	3,402	335	1,179	9,019	741	3,129
Western white pine	610	195	0	200	172	463	83	113	0	892	480	463
Whitebark pine	5	94	0	0	0	0	0	0	0	5	94	0
Total softwoods	64,088	24,231	16,771	54,392	10,890	110,839	159,651	42,282	159,877	278,131	77,403	287,487
Hardwoods:												
Bigleaf maple	64	99	0	0	0	0	0	0	0	64	99	0
Black cottonwood	147	22	0	147	123	0	3,471	1,515	0	3,766	1,660	0
Cherry	0	0	0	0	0	0	185	55	0	185	55	0
Oregon white oak	0	0	0	192	250	318	283	139	0	475	389	318
Quaking aspen	133	595	0	0	0	0	1,661	2,010	349	1,794	2,605	349
Red alder	923	534	0	0	0	0	0	0	0	923	534	0
Western paper birch	219	283	0	479	443	229	527	520	0	1,224	1,247	229
Willow	140	268	0	187	96	0	698	16	0	1,025	379	0
Total hardwoods	1,626	1,801	0	1,006	911	547	6,823	4,256	349	9,455	6,968	896
All species	65,714	26,032	16,771	55,398	11,801	111,386	166,474	46,537	160,226	287,587	84,371	288,383
SE for total (%)	11	14	32	15	18	21	6	9	16	5	7	12

Note: totals may be off because of rounding; data subject to sampling error; SE = sampling error.

0 = less than 500 cubic feet found.

Includes growing-stock trees (noncull trees of commercial species) 5.0 inches in d.b.h. and larger.

Table 24—Estimated gross annual growth, average annual mortality, and average annual removals of sawtimber on non-national-forest timberland, by species and owner class, eastern Washington, January 1, 2002

Thousand board feet, Scribner rule

Species	Other public			Forest industry			Other private			All owners		
	Current gross annual growth	Average annual mortality	Average annual removals	Current gross annual growth	Average annual mortality	Average annual removals	Current gross annual growth	Average annual mortality	Average annual removals	Current gross annual growth	Average annual mortality	Average annual removals
Softwoods:												
Douglas-fir	159,933	43,887	34,797	147,720	15,419	297,431	378,977	56,134	285,823	686,630	115,441	618,051
Engelmann spruce	9,797	8,993	0	2,358	29	2,778	11,887	3,151	0	24,042	12,173	2,778
Grand fir	53,709	19,090	9,713	25,581	8,518	65,424	80,984	39,030	188,000	160,274	66,639	263,137
Lodgepole pine	20,831	8,334	5,010	6,622	3,425	30,484	51,126	18,666	33,816	78,579	30,425	69,310
Mountain hemlock	0	0	0	0	0	0	1,215	24	0	1,215	24	0
Pacific silver fir	0	0	0	0	0	0	668	1,466	0	668	1,466	0
Ponderosa pine	45,532	8,851	9,746	40,237	5,256	75,537	245,338	35,313	215,379	331,107	49,420	300,662
Subalpine fir	7,585	2,009	0	0	0	2,822	3,443	2,490	0	11,027	4,499	2,822
Western hemlock	729	12	0	2,902	344	4,451	4,191	1,248	0	7,822	1,603	4,451
Western larch	13,940	9,183	6,515	6,372	4,063	39,148	44,941	13,215	27,935	65,253	26,461	73,599
Western redcedar	11,277	987	3,631	14,023	513	4,460	13,273	949	5,551	38,573	2,449	13,642
Western white pine	4,205	1,154	0	1,215	891	2,448	370	472	0	5,789	2,517	2,448
Whitebark pine	32	497	0	0	0	0	0	0	0	32	497	0
Total softwoods	327,569	102,996	69,410	247,031	38,459	524,984	836,412	172,158	756,505	1,411,012	313,614	1,350,900
Hardwoods:												
Bigleaf maple	373	343	0	0	0	0	0	0	0	373	3430	0
Black cottonwood	0	0	0	468	628	0	7,669	4,161	0	8,137	4,7890	0
Cherry	0	0	0	0	0	0	0	0	0	0	0	0
Oregon white oak	0	0	0	67	223	0	0	0	0	67	223	0
Quaking aspen	912	2,428	0	0	0	0	5,716	4,824	0	6,628	7,252	0
Red alder	1,694	1,119	0	0	0	0	0	0	0	1,694	1,119	0
Western paper birch	192	197	0	0	0	0	361	501	0	553	698	0
Willow	7,743	487	0	0	0	0	0	0	0	7,743	487	0
Total hardwoods	10,914	4,574	0	535	851	0	13,747	9,486	0	25,196	14,911	0
All species	338,484	107,570	69,410	247,566	39,310	524,984	850,159	181,645	756,505	1,436,208	328,525	1,350,900
SE for total (%)	12	15	33	17	21	21	8	10	17	6	8	12

Note: totals may be off because of rounding; data subject to sampling error; SE = sampling error.

0 = less than 500 board feet found

Includes softwood sawtimber trees 9.0 inches in d.b.h. and larger, and hardwood sawtimber trees 11.0 inches in d.b.h. and larger.

Table 25—Estimated changes in area of non-national-forest timberland by owner class, eastern Washington, 1990-91 to 2002

Description of change	Other public	Forest industry	Other private	All owners Total	SE
	- - - - - - - - - *Thousand acres*				%
Timberland area published in 1990-91	764	878	2,366	4,008	
New estimate of timberland area for 1990-91, based on remeasured plots only	761	884	2,292	3,938	
Area change due to:					
Change caused by new reserve definition	-50	0	129	79	
Changes in inventory area—					
To national forest	-4	-53	0	-57	28
From national forest	0	6	0	6	77
To reserved	-16	0	0	-16	
Net change	-21	-47	0	-68	
Changes in land class—					
Timberland to rights-of-way	0	0	-22	-22	71
Changes in ownership—					
From other public	0	0	0	0	0
From forest industry	11	-106	95	0	31
From other private	29	98	-127	0	31
Net change	40	-8	-32	0	
Timberland area in 2002	731	829	2,367	3,927	
SE for total (%)	6	8	4	2	

Note: totals may be off because of rounding; data subject to sampling error; SE = sampling error.

SE for ownership was calculated for the negative values.

0 = less than 500 acres found.

Negative values are losses of timberland, and positive values are gains of timberland.

Values in this table were derived from a survey unit level stratification and differ slightly from values in other tables in this report.

Owner was updated for some plots, contributing to differences in estimates by owner in 1991.

Table 26—Estimated changes in net volume of growing stock on non-national-forest timberland by species group and owner class, eastern Washington, 1990-91 to 2002

Description	Softwood species				Hardwood species				All species	
	Other public	Forest industry	Other private	All owners	Other public	Forest industry	Other private	All owners	Total	SE
	Million cubic feet									%
Volume published in 1990-91	2,155	2,005	4,858	9,018	68	27	182	277	9,295	
Estimate of 1990-91 volume, based on remeasured plots only	2,392	1,806	4,855	9,053	90	19	157	266	9,319	
Volume changes due to:										
Change in reserve definition	-176	0	456	280	-32	0	8	-24	256	
Changes in inventory area—										
To national forest	-30	-153	0	-183	0	0	0	0	-183	51
From national forest	0	28	0	28	0	0	0	0	28	102
To reserved	-84	0	0	-84	-2	0	0	-2	-86	
Net change	-115	-125	0	-240	-2	0	0	-2	-241	
Changes in land class—										
Timberland to rights-of-way	0	0	-55	-55	0	0	-19	-19	-74	97
Changes in ownership—										
From other public	0	0	0	0	0	0	0	0	0	
From forest industry	8	-170	161	0	0	0	0	0	0	42
From other private	57	239	-297	0	0	13	-13	0	0	35
Net change	66	70	-135	0	0	13	-13	0	0	
Growth, mortality, and harvest—										
Periodic gross growth	591	724	1,824	3,139	14	12	57	83	3,222	5
Periodic mortality	-179	-128	-407	-714	-12	-2	-28	-41	-756	10
Periodic removals	-173	-1,179	-1,626	-2,978	0	-6	-7	-13	-2,991	11
Net change	239	-584	-208	-554	2	4	23	29	-525	
Total volume in 2002	2,406	1,167	4,912	8,485	59	36	155	250	8,735	5
SE for total (%)	12	15	7	5	44	38	44	30	5	

Note: totals may be off because of rounding; data subject to sampling error; SE = sampling error; for ownership, SE was calculated for the sum of the negative values.

0 = less than 500,000 cubic feet found.

Includes growing-stock trees (noncull trees of commercial species) 5.0 inches in d.b.h. and larger; negative values result from loss of timberland, mortality, or removals.

Owner was updated for some plots, contributing to differences in estimates by owner in 1991.

Table 27—Estimated changes in net volume of sawtimber on non-national-forest timberland by species group and owner class, eastern Washington, 1990-91 to 2002

Description	Softwood species				Hardwood species				All species	
	Other public	Forest industry	Other private	All owners	Other public	Forest industry	Other private	All owners	Total	SE
	Million board feet, Scriber rule									*%*
Volume published in 1990-91	9,284	8,473	19,810	37,566	221	62	488	770	38,336	
Estimate of 1990-91 volume, based on remeasured plots only	11,266	7,284	19,843	38,393	411	8	294	714	39,107	
Volume changes due to: Change in reserve definition	-697	0	2,054	1,357	-139	0	10	-129	1,229	
Changes in inventory area—										
To national forest	-144	-630	0	-773	0	0	0	0	-773	54
From national forest	0	134	0	134	0	0	0	0	134	100
To reserved	-1,080	0	0	-1,080	-139	0	0	-139	-1,219	
Net change	-1,224	-496	0	-1,720	-139	0	0	-139	-1,859	73
Changes in land class—										
Timberland to rights-of-way	0	0	-235	-235	0	0	-73	-73	-308	73
Changes in ownership—										
From other public	0	0	0	0	0	0	0	0	0	
From forest industry	28	-791	763	0	0	0	0	0	0	45
From other private	143	848	-991	0	0	17	-17	0	0	34
Net change	171	57	-228	0	0	17	-17	0	0	
Growth, mortality, and harvest—										
Periodic gross growth	2,880	3,560	9,268	15,707	56	5	160	220	15,928	5
Periodic mortality	-656	-364	-1,451	-2,471	-43	0	-24	-66	-2,537	12
Periodic removals	-718	-5,592	-7,725	-14,035	0	0	-15	-15	-14,050	12
Net change	1,506	-2,397	92	-798	13	5	121	139	-659	
Total volume in 2002	11,022	4,448	21,526	36,997	147	30	335	513	37,509	
SE for total (%)	14	16	8	6	55	77	48	35	6	

Note: totals may be off because of rounding; data subject to sampling error; SE = sampling error; for ownership, SE was calculated for the sum of the negative values.
0 = less than 500,000 board feet found.
Includes softwood sawtimber trees 9.0 inches in d.b.h. and larger, and hardwood sawtimber trees 11.0 inches in d.b.h. and larger.
Owner was updated for some plots, contributing to differences in estimates by owner in 1991.

Table 28—Estimated sawtimber harvest volume by year and owner class, eastern Washington, 1955-2001

Year	National forest	Other public	Private	All owners
		Thousand board feet, Scribner rule		
1955	172,714	47,673	537,955	758,342
1956	217,290	46,097	504,073	767,460
1957	227,845	37,657	485,045	750,547
1958	250,764	29,131	491,670	771,565
1959	330,307	35,716	536,507	902,530
1960	272,884	29,195	536,180	838,259
1961	288,501	27,229	481,854	797,584
1962	400,062	37,159	454,426	891,647
1963	411,925	41,419	491,028	944,372
1964	427,596	38,232	547,882	1,013,710
1965	433,090	75,941	530,562	1,039,593
1966	428,176	75,922	526,794	1,030,892
1967	448,802	84,539	531,740	1,065,081
1968	472,669	102,260	603,772	1,178,701
1969	426,409	118,017	523,715	1,068,141
1970	332,863	67,014	490,807	890,684
1971	385,967	110,434	573,711	1,070,112
1972	481,759	91,899	615,658	1,189,316
1973	439,170	113,300	666,398	1,218,868
1974	382,870	76,699	683,056	1,142,625
1975	339,847	66,583	606,463	1,012,893
1976	363,896	78,859	689,188	1,131,943
1977	321,884	116,758	730,581	1,169,223
1978	339,443	108,993	771,153	1,219,589
1979	291,369	89,186	747,201	1,127,756
1980	316,864	55,485	686,626	1,058,975
1981	297,105	51,486	585,130	933,721
1982	178,788	23,331	525,473	727,592
1983	399,356	92,725	634,084	1,126,165
1984	327,596	123,010	597,153	1,047,759
1985	324,138	96,516	683,390	1,104,044
1986	396,551	108,974	718,637	1,224,162
1987	462,312	146,022	729,928	1,338,262
1988	426,280	121,557	748,721	1,296,558
1989	433,511	119,929	805,671	1,359,111
1990	313,259	102,628	759,905	1,175,792
1991	284,304	68,673	737,433	1,090,410
1992	205,206	58,175	799,594	1,062,975
1993	160,975	68,012	793,654	1,022,641
1994	85,664	48,561	787,700	921,925
1995	71,306	96,337	807,793	975,436
1996	147,407	107,802	822,891	1,078,100
1997	105,281	97,482	786,045	988,808
1998	58,681	77,859	755,708	892,248
1999	70,749	89,482	847,700	1,007,931
2000	59,743	89,741	803,309	952,793
2001	61,332	73,633	739,183	874,148

Source: Washington timber harvest reports, Washington Department of Natural Resources.

Appendix

The field plots selected for the 2001 inventory of eastern Washington consisted of 742 forest and nonforest field locations established in previous inventories. These plots were systematically selected to represent three-fifths of the base inventory grid sampled in 1990. To ensure adequate representation of forest and nonforest plots in each county, the selection of plots was done by dividing the plots in the 1990 inventory into forest and nonforest categories, sorting by county and plot number, and sequentially selecting every first, third, and fifth plot in each group of five sorted plots.

Examination of inventory results (specifically table 25) indicated that the new estimate of timberland in 1990 (3,938,000 acres) was lower than the estimate reported in McKay et al. (1995) (4,008,000 acres). All area estimates and inventory procedures were double-checked for errors. It was found, as shown in the table below, that simply by chance, the systematic selection resulted in a slightly different ratio of number of timberland to total number of plots in 2001 (0.439) than in 1990 (0.449).

| | 1990 | | 2001 | | |
Land type	Number of plots	Ratio to total plots	Number of plots	Ratio to total plots	Adjusted number of plots
Timberland	560	0.449	326	0.439	326
Other forest	118	.095	76	.102	69
Nonforest	568	.456	340	.458	331
All	1,246		742		726

Since the field measurement had already been completed and a few years had already passed, it was not possible to adjust the selection and measure additional timberland plots to match the ratio in the 1990 sample. However, it was possible to randomly drop other forest and nonforest plots from the 2001 data to match the 1990 timberland-to-total plots ratio. For example, using 69 of the 76 other forest plots and 331 of the 340 nonforest plots.

Although adjusting the grid after the fact would arguably result in inventory results that were a more accurate reflection of change since 1990, adjusting a sample after examining problematic results introduces a direct bias into the inventory that was not there with the original sample. In addition, the effect was relatively minor, and the difference between the new estimate of timberland in 1990 and the one reported in McKay et al. (1995), 70,000 acres, was still within one standard error of the estimate (SE = 80,000 acres). The decision was made to not adjust the selected plots in the inventory. However, the result of the (potentially) more accurate adjusted inventory, and those published in this report, could be of interest, and selected results for tables 25 through 27 are compared in the table below.

Value	Units	Unadjusted	Adjusted
New estimate of timberland area for 1990-91, based on remeasured plots only	Thousand acres	3,938	3,980
Timberland area in 2002	Thousand acres	3,927	3,968
Estimate of 1990-91 volume, based on remeasured plots only	Million cubic feet	9,319	9,386
Total volume in 2002	Million cubic feet	8,735	8,805
Estimate of 1990-91 volume, based on remeasured plots only	Million board feet, Scribner rule	39,107	39,356
Total volume in 2002	Million board feet, Scribner rule	37,509	37,788

www.ingramcontent.com/pod-product-compliance
Lightning Source LLC
Chambersburg PA
CBHW080552290526
45790CB00006B/2632